About the Author

Caitlin Kent-Halliday is a twenty-year-old poet from South London. At eighteen, inspired by her own self-discovery journey, grief, and navigating through the start of womanhood and over all trials and triumphs of life, Caitlin began to write *Peace of Mind* as a way of finding inner peace and joy. With the hopes it will do the same for others.

caitlinkenthalliday.com

Peace of Mind

Caitlin Kent-Halliday

Peace of Mind

Olympia Publishers
London

www.olympiapublishers.com
OLYMPIA PAPERBACK EDITION

Copyright © Caitlin Kent-Halliday 2024

The right of Caitlin Kent-Halliday to be identified as author of this work has been asserted in accordance with sections 77 and 78 of the Copyright, Designs and Patents Act 1988.

All Rights Reserved

No reproduction, copy or transmission of this publication may be made without written permission.
No paragraph of this publication may be reproduced, copied or transmitted save with the written permission of the publisher, or in accordance with the provisions of the Copyright Act 1956 (as amended).

Any person who commits any unauthorised act in relation to this publication may be liable to criminal prosecution and civil claims for damage.

A CIP catalogue record for this title is available from the British Library.

ISBN: 978-1-80439-956-9

This is a work of fiction.
Names, characters, places and incidents originate from the writer's imagination. Any resemblance to actual persons, living or dead, is purely coincidental.

First Published in 2024

Olympia Publishers
Tallis House
2 Tallis Street
London
EC4Y 0AB

Printed in Great Britain

Dedication

For my mum, you may no longer be here, but you are always with me. I love you. 'Ai Shiteru'

Acknowledgements

Thank you to my beautiful Nanny Phil for always being at the other end of the phone to listen to all I write. I wouldn't be the woman I am today, without you.

Thank you to Peg, who sparked my love for literature and the power it possesses.

Thank you, Kacper, for being the first reader of 'Peace of Mind,' your opinion is valued. *The world needs more people like you.*

Thank you to Sara, for the book cover photography.

Part One:
Hurt

Kiss the Rose

'Kiss the rose,' he said,
but as my lips touched the woven thread, they bled.

Thorns dug deep into my skin; he wore a devil's grin.

Learning to swallow my pride; believe me, I've tried to fight,
but you crawl back to him.

You watched but never cared,
as I cried upon the blood–stained armchair.

You're telling me you're lonely,
and you never meant to hurt me;
well, then why did you leave me?

Why did you leave me?

I'm tired of taking all the blame.
Those stupid words, stay the same;
I know you'll never change.

Listen

Listen,
before you drift
off into another dimension
because the invention
of the thoughts in our heads,
will surely shred us to the bone.

Listen,
you do not possess a heart of stone;
you have shown
it's possible to find our way,
in this mess, we call home.

Listen,
before the annual gloam settles upon us,
cut loose from the fear of tomorrow.
Look forward and seldom back at a world gone,
blind, bleak,
and oh, so black.

Protective Mechanism

If I don't let them hold me,
they cannot let me go.

Grief

Sometimes I'm fine; and then I'm not.

The grief punches me in the face; rips out my guts,
and leaves them on the floor.

The uncontrollable pain,
floods my body.

All I can do is wait
for this torture to pass, so the cycle
can start
again.

Conversation Mouse Traps

Mouse traps are laced through every conversation I have.

A light-hearted question has just been asked,
by this person I'm only just getting to know.
I have been caught.

I contemplate lying
to avoid turning this light-hearted conversation heavy,
causing it to fall to the floor.

I know this escape would only be temporary
I cannot hide from my reality forever;
but right now changing my narrative
would make my life easier.

I dread the awkward silence
and avoidance of eye contact,
that often follows exposing the truth.

It feels wrong to lie;
but this conversation is on the brink
of going deeper then feels comfortable
with someone I barely know.

I should have stayed inside
or when I tell the truth,
I wish I'd lied.

The Insignificance of Material Things

You can still cry
in a Tiffany necklace.

Pins, Pricks and ICKs

Falling in love with you was like sticking pins in my eyes;
it was both painful, and I was blinded,
unable to see what was right in front of me.

The idea of being with you did not match the reality;
although sweet at first, you soon grew bitter,
you treated me like a piece of litter.

I naively believed you were a dove,
when in fact you are a duck.
It was clear you just wanted to Fu*k.

I have woken up from the trance you had me in
and realise you're a prick;
you now you give me the ICK.

Brain Fog

My mind has gone blank; there's a million things
I could be doing,
a thousand things I should be doing,
but my soul feels dead.

Sending messages feels hard; the words aren't forming,
I am falling
into a pit of numbness,
I don't know when I'll get out.

When my body functions,
it feels wrong, forced, and unnatural;
I walk around like a corpse,
put on red lipstick
and a smile when needed.

The Hold You Had on Me

Something told me loving you was a mistake;
but I wanted you to ruin me, as twisted as that seems.

Worldly Disconnect

I have fallen out of love with the world;
despite its occasional beauty, to be at war with it
is not a battle
I'm willing to begin.

Either side, I'm sure I'd feel the same,
as I glide in and out
of this constant disdain.

Sing Loud Scream Louder

Down the motorway, the music was loud,
but we sang louder.
I thought I knew you then.

My love for you has since died.
It lays cold and still, poisoned by your cruelty;
it cannot be revived.

Your arms, once warm, grew cold,
you wore me down till I was nothing.

To you, I was prey to be hunted and placed in a cage;
so I ran fast and screamed louder.

Now I am free,
you will never control me.

Conditional Love

His words do not match his actions; our love has terms,
I cannot live in these conditions.
The heat is rising,
fire is catching,
and the smoke will not clear
with his meaningless sentiments.

Rolling Stone

My life did not pause when you left;
I continued to live through pain and grief
in your absence.

What makes you think
you can treat your daughter this way,
when all I wanted was for you to stay.

You think you can treat me like shit;
but I will not put up with it.
I am worth more than you bargained me for.

Fickle

Are you who you portray yourself to be?
Your fickle friendship is a waste of energy;
lately, you've shown me your reality.

I was in your corner there at any moment,
but you dropped me when it was convenient;
you have become despondent.

To you, I poured out my soul;
but you are not who you sold yourself to be.
I feel exposed;
you've disposed of me.

Narcissism

Free to have an opinion,
but only if it was yours.
Free to live as I pleased,
but not if it displeased you.

Come to think of it, I was not free at all.

I was your priority
until you found someone new;
I was the one,
you came crying to.

Your hateful words drove me insane;
you told me I was not sane.
Your hateful words
would disappear from your memory;
but will forever linger in mine.

Outside Looking In

In panic, I step outside myself; my soul leaves me.
I have become someone I don't recognise,
but I have seen it many times before.

As a prisoner of overwhelm, you are stuck.
Mental unrest has its hands around your neck;
you gasp for air, but nothing enters your lungs.
You feel this must be it; your body is caving in.
Nerves pulse through you, but they do not register.
You lay there pulsating, barely alive, just existing.

Why Did You Bother?

I don't miss you,
I miss the way you made me feel.
You made me believe you wanted me;
and now you're acting as if I don't exist.

Undressing Me with Your Eyes

I am dressed from head to toe;
here you are, undressing me with your eyes.
You look me up and down,
and just like that, I feel disgraced.

To you, I am flesh for you to devour,
nothing more than a weak flower.
Little do you know, I am no shrinking violet;
and there you are thinking,
you have a right to touch me.

Like Clay

Like clay, you moulded me;
your rough hands reshaped me.
Changing every precious detail to please your eye;
but the kiln was too hot and I fell apart.

Gas to a Flame

I'm your number one,
but I feel like an afterthought.
When you've pushed everyone else away,
I'm your last resort.

Having you around is like putting gas to a flame;
the world burns until all that remains is ash.
You rip lives to shreds,
then you'll turn around and say, you did it all for me.

You Cannot Always Need What You Love

I have come to learn that love can either be the thing
that lifts us or
tears us down.

It's cruel the way love can build you up high
only so when the foundations break, you have further to fall.

It's impossible to see which direction it's heading;
sometimes, love can turn,
and you only realise it broke you, when you're on the floor
putting your life back together.

Simply due to the sweet nothings they had you believe,
and the empty promises you built your life around.

Cat Caller

There was no need for you to honk at me;
I already felt your hungry glare,
before you brought your existence to my attention,
with that degrading action.
When you boys have daughters,
maybe then you'll become men,
or is that just wishful thinking?

You may howl,
but you cannot touch me.
I should have worn a longer skirt;
maybe then they wouldn't look my way.

But I wore a skirt down to my ankles yesterday,
and the glares and grins persisted.
I'm a confident woman;
but when I feel their eyes on me,
I want the ground to eat me,
and my walking pace seems to slow down.

I know a good man is out there;
one that will call me a goddess.
A man that won't treat me like his mistress,
nothing more than to body to undress.

But for now, I feel deflated.

No one warned me with womanhood
came the gaze from a stranger,
that hangs his head out a van window like a dog drooling.

Trying to Save You from Yourself

I'm telling you,
that you can't save others from themselves;
and yet here I am,
trying to save you from yourself.

Something from Your Nothing

I thought if I tolerated your sh*t for long enough,
love would flourish;
but I was naïve, thinking,
Something could come from your nothing.

How could I have known?
Your affections turned me colour-blind;
all the red flags looked green.
I was only taking in what was in front of me,
but you changed just as quickly as you came.

Substitution Demons

Use alcohol to cope with what troubles you,
and it ends up being part of the problem.
Addiction is a demon that you can't fight off.

It pretends to be your friend, stabs you in the back
with a freshly sharpened blade, and has you convinced,
they are needed in order to survive.
Only to leave you alone and wounded.

A demon you see as a lifeline,
that cuts your lifetime short;
and blinds you from seeing
the abundance of love that surrounds you.

Generational Backache

My back ached
from a lifetime of distress.
I could no longer carry the burden
of all that came before;
I felt it wearing down my bones,
till I become weak and unable to stand.

Sacrifices to Satisfy

He did not love me;
he loved who I became to satisfy him,
out of fear of displeasing him.

I did not love him;
I loved the man he pretended to be to trick me,
to give a false sense of security.

Bone Dry Oasis

Will someone please
get me out of this oasis?
My head is spinning, and I am far from safety.

The promise of water brought me here,
but this arena is bone dry.
If I'm left here much longer, I'm not sure
I'll make it out alive.

Near but Far

You're in front of me;
and yet you're miles away,
your eyes are glazed.

I'm talking directly to you;
but I can see right through you,
It's like I'm talking to a window pane.

Confessions

The act of confessing our sins alone
will not rectify what is broken.
Only through actions will we have a chance
of reviving what was lost.

Dishonour

How can you expect
all you mistreat to honour your word,
to stick by you through
thick and thin?

Do you not see the cause of your actions?
The destruction will not go away,
simply because you tell me
it was never there in the first place.

Robbing Me Blind of My Rationality

What was it about you
that made me put down my defences,
and throw my heart right into the middle of the battlefield?

I should have listened to Amy when she told me:
Love is a losing game.

I gambled it all
and placed my bets on you;
but as the cards were drawn, you were the joker,
robbing me blind of my rationality.

Trip Hazard

In this family, there is more than an elephant in the room,
but an entire zoo.

There comes a point where it's just impossible to ignore.
The lump under the carpet is so large,
that it becomes a trip hazard.
One of these days,
someone is bound to fall on their face.

Emotional Sinus

I was clogged up with stress; I could feel it accumulating,
causing me to put my head in my hands.

I scrunched up my face,
as if that would squeeze the heaviness out of my brain.
My jaw was clenched;
my shoulders were hunched,
emotional sinus was weighing me down.

Ignored

You only listen
if I say what you want to hear.
You won't even look me in the eye.

Everything and Nothing All at Once

I have everything,
and nothing to give simultaneously.
My brain is about to burst at the seams;
but I get moments where I can't move.
Yet here I am moving.
Somewhere and nowhere all at once.

I wish to be seen
but have never been so desperate to hide.
These contradictions engulf me;
and yet, they spit me out alive every time.
Determination is what keeps me alive.

If only learning to not love you,
was as easy
as loving you.

No Longer Here to Hold

It haunts me that your hands are no longer here to hold,
that I'll never hear your gentle voice.
I could always hear
the ache in your words.
I wanted more than anything to take it all away.

Love-Ish

It's not that I want you in my life, but you left your mark.
Since you turned your back,
I gave myself the time to process
the overwhelming emotion that pursued me;
and turned it into the strength,
that drives me to pursue my desires.

I still have memories to navigate though;
it's not easy for my brain to forget about you.
It is strange to think you once held my hand,
and now the very thought of that I cannot stand.

This was never about picking a side;
all I wanted was for you to see things,
from my point of view.

I still talk as if I saw you yesterday
and think of the times we spent together;
but instead of bringing me joy, they make my heart ache.

I Am Lonely without You
[Anata ga inakute samishī desu]

I am what you left behind;
and just as your blood flows through my veins,
my blood once flowed through yours.
I am lonely without you.
Countless times I fought the urge to call you,
to say all the things
that were left unsaid.
Then I remember you are gone
and cry instead.

I am lonely without you.
Anata ga inakute samishī desu。

Backwards

It feels wrong
that it was cold when you passed, and in the time gone by,
the days have gotten hot.
How backward,
for the sun to shine without you here.

Bad Dream

I thought I'd run out of things to say,
but I still remember
the sound of your voice, as if I heard it yesterday.

I want to escape this twisted nightmare,
that I hope to wake up from;
and when I awake
you'll be there to tell me,
it was just a bad dream.

Dodgy Paths

I get apprehensive about letting my heart lead the way;
it's been led down
some pretty dodgy paths.

Flame to Fire, Fire to Flame

A flame brings light in darkness and warmth in the cold.
It possesses a mesmerising beauty.

As a symbol of hope and remembrance,
it's easy to forget if you touched it,
it would burn you.

In a split second,
a flame can turn into fire;
untamed, destroying everything in its wake.

Once a flame turns to fire, it cannot be reversed.
You can only put out the raging fire that now exists;
and light a new candle with an understanding,
of how to protect your precious flame.

Sea of Suffering

There is comfort in knowing
we are not alone in our struggles;
but when I think about the people I love
experiencing the same tormenting emotions
as I have at some point in my life,
my heart becomes heavy.
The thought alone,
makes my stomach churn.

Knowing that I cannot fight their battles for them,
I can only stand by their side.
When I would take
the cuff of pain as it floods their way,
so, they would not drown
in a sea of suffering.

They Call You Grief

You arrived on a morning as cold as your heart,
ready to rip my life apart.

You sent no warning of your arrival,
nor did you knock on the door.
You just left me crying
on my living room floor.

You sat with me at every table and captured my soul,
with no intention of giving it back without a fight.

No word in the human language can truly describe
the torture you inflict;
but they call you grief.

Small Picture

It's easy to believe
a life you are not living is better than your own.

Especially when solely viewed within the bounds,
of your phone.

The Dip

It happens so quickly, the dip.
It's like I'm floating, yet everything weighs a ton.
I know it will pass; it always does.
In the meantime,
I will use what willpower I have left
and listen to the voice within me that says:
'No, don't give up yet.'

The Words You Didn't Say

Somehow
It's the words you didn't say that hurt the most.
Not the words you said.

Part Two:
Heal

Start of Healing

I am breaking my silence.
No longer will my past dominate me.

I am responsible for where I go from here;
but that is a blessing,
you only ever dragged me through hell.

My Mother's Heart

There is nothing like a mother's love
our heartbeats were once intertwined; we are one,
with every beat of her heart, I was soothed.

Albeit a messy love, the hardship failed to break it,
only leaving cracks,
that we were learning to fix.

Now she is gone;
I feel her presence
in the sun's rays as it shines upon the world,
I know she still lives within me.

When I put my hand on my chest,
it's as if her heart beats within mine.
She is always with me.

Mascara Stain on My Bed Sheets

I was fine;
but now there's a mascara stain on my bed sheets,
and I've disconnected from my senses.
I'll lay here to let the disconnect wash over me;
my determination remains somewhere within me.
As long as I am breathing, I can find myself again.
I may feel powerless,
but I'll take one small step, knowing that one step forward
is better than no steps at all.

False Reflections

How others treat you,
is not always a reflection
of how you deserve to be treated.

Let Them Lose You

If they let you go when it suits them, let them lose you;
let them sit with the choices they have made.
Don't waste another second
trying to convince them of your worth;
It will only leave you with nothing left to give,
let them lose you.

I Forgive but Can't Forget

I forgive but can't forget;
for it's the memory of the pain you caused me
that lingers in my head.

Though forgiveness,
I free myself from living in hatred;
as I know it takes too much of my soul.

A part of me that could be put into making my life shine
a little brighter, even in my darkest hours
when the pain floods my heart.

Like a tide, it comes in waves,
there's no way of knowing how hard it hits;
but I know I will not go down on a sinking ship.

Source of Suffering

There is power in identifying the source of your suffering;
only then can you heal from what torments you.

It won't dissipate immediately,
but its power over you will loosen.
It may sit in the back of your mind,
and sting you when you least expect;
but if you've risen above it once,
you can rise again.

The Ego Is Never Full [Ghosted]

You ghosted me, but to you,
I was the invisible one.

You'd tare me down
on the pursuit
of building yourself higher;
but I will no longer let your ego
feed on my soul.

For the ego is never full;
it would keep feasting
till there was not a morsel of me left.

True Embodiment

Where you are from
does not make you who you are;
you decide who you get to be.

Through active steps, you embody your true self.
Never let the soulless mould you,
into someone, you are not.

Why would you waste your life
being a false version of yourself, just to keep the peace?
You think it's easier to play along
the truth is, it never lasts.

The world needs you as you are;
not the version of yourself
you thought you had to be
to be accepted.

I Know You're Tired But...

I know you're tired,
but your life is worth the fight.
This is not like the endless battles
you've fought before.

This time you're fighting for the life you deserve;
the freedom you've always longed for.
Time has broken you,
but wounds heal with time.

Beauty in Our Broken

I found beauty in our broken;
and said goodbye with forgiveness in my heart,
I had forgotten how loved
I once felt in your arms.

I remembered the days
you'd braid flowers in my hair,
and leave heart-shaped notes by my bedside.

You were the one who taught me how to love;
and just how easily it can be taken away.

I didn't know that would be the last time we'd talk;
it's hard to remember all that was said,
but in the words we shared,
we found peace in our pain.

Power in the Present Moment

When dreaming of what you wish to achieve in the future, remember it is what you do in the present
that will lead you there.

I Wish My Mother Never Met My Father

Sometimes I wish my mother never met my father;
I think of all the pain she would have avoided,
the life she could have had
without my father treating her like crap on his shoe.

I wish that my mother had the chance to grow old
with someone who loved her;
someone who treated her right,
but then it dawns on me:
I would not exist if that were reality.

Then something fires up within me;
a feeling greater than hatred and beyond resentment.
A want to make the torture she faced loving him worth it,
I desire to be something right among the wrong.

Safety Nest

My parents left the nest before I did;
loved me and left me lonely.
So I taught myself how to fly
and leave all they left behind.
To build a nest of my own;
a safety nest to call my home.

Soul

Those who do not act upon their soul wishes in life,
are often burdened
with an overwhelming sense of unhappiness;
due to an unsatisfied part of themselves,
and the gap a want without action tends to leave.

This stresses,
the importance of connection from within
that curates a deeper understanding,
of what we truly desire to be.
In effect, this quiets the numbing external noise;
that tends to cloud our judgement,
make us fear our true identity;
and ignore our true capabilities.

Expectation of Self

I filter through what others expect of me,
to find what I expect of myself.
I will not waste time
trying to live up to someone's unrealistic ideals,
of what my life has to be.
I can only live by the standards I set for myself;
formulated through a deep understanding,
of what I am truly capable of.

A Life without Discussion

A difference in opinion is not a weakness;
duality sparks discussions that lead to expansion.
We then possess a greater understanding
of the concepts we both agree and disagree on;
to reach beyond what we thought was possible.
A life without discussion is simply pointless.
A life without discussion restricts the mind.

The Negative Has to Be Seen

You cannot just look at the positive;
sometimes negatives have to be seen.
If you ignore what is wrong
you cannot put it right;
it is when we acknowledge what is deceitful,
a deeper understanding of what is pure is gained.

Mistakes Don't Formulate Bad Habits

Don't let your mistakes formulate bad habits;
break the cycle, cover the ditch before it gets deeper;
climb out, clean off the decay and keep going.
There's no need to hit self-destruct;
you will only fall further down;
you are needed here above the soil.

Would You Let This Man Raise Your Child?

If you think he's the one, ask yourself:
Do I want this man in my children's life?
Even if you don't see motherhood in your future
ask yourself:
Would you let this man raise your child?
If the answer is no, then he's not the one.

Pain Knows No Boundary

Pain is not a living thing it has no heart nor flesh;
it makes no noise to warn you of its arrival,
it simply creeps up on you.

Pain knows no boundary;
and cannot distinguish between good and evil.
Therefore, the pain you face is not based
on a judgement of your character.

On the Days I Don't Know Myself

You know me on the days I don't know myself;
you see right through my still exeter,
and see the life hidden beneath.

You hold my hand
to let me know you're there;
to remind me I am loved,
even though I can't bear to hear it.

Phantom Devil Horns

Like all humans, you were born pure;
a spirit untouched by emotional manipulation,
nothing had entered your mind or damaged your being.
You could sense and feel,
but you were not yet able to go beyond,
persecutions of life that were external to yourself.

As you got older, you climbed further up the hairs of life
all too soon, exposed, you began to over analyse
and overcompensate.

Dragging down your once-untouched soul,
they called you a homewrecker, a monster, and a burden
for simply existing.
It became hard to disconnect yourself,
from the abuse that was thrown your way.

You were only a child,
when you looked in the mirror, you saw horns;
but now you are older, you can regain control,
you never lost your true nature despite all that was said.

Understand you are not defined,
by other people's opinion of you;
connect with yourself again and you will see
you are not the devil they painted you out to be.

What Do You Need?

You need yourself more than I need you.
I want you;
but understand, needs come before wants.

There are people, beating you down
because they want too much from you.
What do you need?

I need you to look after yourself;
find the door to your desires,
find yourself again.

When you need me
I'll be here with open arms,
and a heart full of love.

Don't worry if you don't
have everything figured out.
You do not have to face your battles alone.

I Am Not, Who I Was

I may tell the story of my past,
but it is the story of who I have become
that matters the most.

The Action of Inaction

Thoughts themselves hold no capabilities;
you decide what to do and what not to do;
deciding not to decide is in itself a decision.
It's the action of inaction,
that decays the soul.

Here and Now

Memory is a simulation formed by our past;
it does not exist in the here and now.
We are living beings, unlike our memories.
They are in the past. We are in the present.
Therefore, we have more power than the events of our past to make a brighter future.

I identify my trauma; but my trauma does not identify me.

My life's purpose,
is not to convince you of my value.

You Know What You Are Worth

When they leave,
when nothing adds up,
and they simply decide when you're convenient.
When they slip in and out of your life as they please,
without considering how you may feel.

Don't let their lack of accountability
be the reason you feel worthless,
when they drop you out of nowhere
with no explanation at all.

You deserve someone
who is not necessarily there at your every beckon call;
but will be there when you fall,
by your side through it all.
It's not too much to ask for.

Love is not words.
Love is action, love is care;
love is kindness, love is being there.

Love isn't walking away when it gets tough.
Love is knowing
you care enough about that person to stay.

Don't stick by someone,

who makes you feel like you're screaming at a brick wall,
that you feel like slamming your head against.

Don't wait around for them to see who you are;
you know who you are.

You know what you are worth.

The Burden of Hatred

Hatred is a burden the heart cannot hold;
yet even when the weight becomes too much to bare,
it begins to hinder our way of life,
it is not so easily shifted.

It's a feeling that burns from inside you;
you feel it as it rises and begins to take over your senses.
It consumes you,
but you must not let it become you.

Sorry Is Not Enough

When I think back to those nights it is not all clear;
it comes back to me in vague imagery and sound.
I remember you standing there above me
dripping with rage;
with your chest puffed up
and your hands placed on your hips.

You stood there looking down at me,
like I was an ant to be crushed.
You were standing close enough
for me to feel the radiation of your anger;
I thought any minute now, you'd punch me.

Those nights don't haunt me like they used to.
If someone was to ask me:
'Would you rub it all away?' I'd say yes,
but the past cannot be erased.

I was not built by my trauma;
but my ability to live beyond it is testament to my strength.
I have spent the years I have lived since
learning to navigate through the flashbacks that arise;
so that they don't manipulate me
like you once did.

I am not the little girl who was defenceless

as you stood glaring at me with disgust
from my bedroom door.
I am now a woman;
who knows her worth in this world,
nothing you could ever say or do
will take that from me.

I Do Not Wish You Suffering

I do not wish you suffering;
the life you have led is punishment enough,
when you waste your life's purpose on tearing others down, it
hurts you more than anyone.

You've wasted your precious time on Earth
making lives a living hell.
Meaning you have not felt any true joy on your own;
you may blame others for your misfortune,
but it was self- inflicted.
There will come a day you'll be out of time,
to put your wrongs to rights.

Number 64

I went back to the street I grew up on;
everything seemed to have shrunk, but then again,
I left a child and have returned a woman.

Six years have passed since I was here last;
I don't even know why I have returned,
maybe it's a longing for closure.
Maybe I thought if I knocked on the door of number 64,
my mother would be there.
As though we'd never left.

'Hey kit kat,' she'd say as I'd run into her arms,
safe in her embrace like no damage had ever been done.

I ventured further down memory lane;
and popped into the corner shop,
a mere two-minute walk away.
Rita noticed me enter, turned her head, and said, 'Caitlin,'
as if time had never shifted;
like I was still the little girl
that used to buy sweets at the till.

The way Rita recognised me was a comfort.
It was evidence of her beautiful soul and observant nature.
I thought I'd have to tell her who I was;
and after all those years, she never forgot me.

She said I was welcome back anytime,
and for that, I am grateful.

On the way back home
I didn't know what to think or feel,
I just let the experience sink in.

The cab driver started a conversation,
and somehow ended up telling me
he'd be working on Christmas Day
because he had no family to spend it with.
Then, it hit me.
I imagined knocking on the door of number 64,
and having dinner with my mum.

The thought festered inside me,
and caused my heart to burn with sadness.
A longing that could never be fulfilled.
I was on my way home,
but it felt like I was driving away from it.

But if there's one thing I know,
sometimes you must let the past go.
I cannot hold on to the idea of family
that faded long ago.
I'll make the next six years,
something future me will be proud of.

Passions Require Patience

Your passion requires patience;
it is the tree that can bear fruit.
If neglected, it will fail to blossom,
nor will it reach its full potential.

The fruits of your dedication will take time to appear;
but life waits for no one,
so live now as you mean to go forward.
And when the sessions are rough,
know that not all is lost.

Fresh Eyes

A year ago, I wasn't able to walk down these streets
without the burden of my past trauma,
seeping through the cracks of my brain.
Affecting my perception of the present,
staining my reality with a blanket of darkness.

And yet here I am with you,
where the grasp of my past cannot reach me;
starting a new way of life.
I feel lost in the crowd, and yet I am found,
as we walk around taking in all that surrounds us.

Not one part the same;
a constant stream of faces I'll never see again.
I have been here many times;
but I'm seeing it all with fresh eyes,
with you by my side.

Your inability to love me,
will not be the reason
I do not love myself.

Empathy

I'm here.
I know that's not always enough
to make all that troubles you, melt away;
but I will stay by your side,
for you to unclog your mind.

I will not tell you to 'just be happy.'
I know if you could,
you would never feel so blue.
You will see this though;
I still see the hope shining through you.

Rose Surrounded by Pricks

Sometimes I feel like I am a rose
surrounded by pricks;
they stick into my luscious stem and leave a mark.

Not even the rich soil
that surrounds my roots
can protect me from such harm.

Only the sun's light,
will heal my wounds.

Reborn

I have been reborn,
learning what it means
to live without you.

I Was Never You

You stood in front of me hollering abuse;
as if you were looking at yourself in the mirror
because the abuse you threw at me,
was not a reflection of me
but of you.

The After Effect

You blame yourself at first,
replay every single conversation you ever had.

Imagine what it would be like to punch them in the face;
so maybe they would feel a speck
of the pain they caused you.

You long to make them pay for the way they had you believe
they were nothing short of perfection;
wonder how the hell did they woke up one day,
and decide you weren't enough.

You'll make endless excuses
to answer all the unanswered questions,
they left you with.
Drive yourself insane over the way
they just won't leave you head,
as quickly as they tried to get into your bed.

'I'll get over it,' you'll say.
But you wonder how many times the heart can break.

You may not think so now,
but the day will come where you'll say,
'What was I thinking,'
and laugh.

They once made you weak in the knees,
now you just want to kick them in the back of theirs;
but you have better ways
to spend your time.

Sun Kisses

If I were to visit my younger self,
when laughter came as easily as breathing;
and the world was yet to be discovered.

I would tell her
that on this Earth of land and sea,
there are creatures lurking where the Sun never shines.

That as she begins to explore, they will rear their heads,
and try to steal her precious light.

'Fresh meat,' they'll say
as they prepare to prance.

But I will also tell her,
never to let her curiosity die.
That even when the Sun is covered by clouds,
one day they will clear,
she will feel the Sun's kiss again.

Peace of Mind

I'll give
a piece of my mind, so we can find,
peace of mind.

Second Nature

It has been a rough few years;
but you are not the creator of the pain,
others have inflicted upon you.
You get to create your life from here onwards.

Look at all you have achieved despite it all;
it has become second nature to you,
to not give up the fight.

The people that try and break you,
have nothing better to do;
you, on the other hand, have dreams to chase.

You are not weak because you cry;
 it is what you do after the tears
that is your power.

Without fail, you rise each morning,
and move your beautiful body;
you strive for what is best for you.

You step outside into the world to face it head-on;
a world that can be cruel enough,
without you being cruel to yourself.

Redemption

When I was little,
you'd sing me a song of redemption;
who knew,
I'd have to escape you.

I was shrinking under your shadow,
for the sun could not reach me.

I needed to feel
the warmth of light,
before I disappeared completely.

'I want you to be independent,' you'd say
with wicked conviction.
In reality,
you wanted me to be dependent.

The mental stress
you caused was too much,
only I could free myself from your clutch
This is my redemption overdue;
I can live my life without you.

Left

I found myself
when you left.

I Cannot Be the One to Change You

I sometimes wonder if you were different,
if you weren't so reckless in your ways.
Would you be by my side today?

Then I remember I cannot be the one
to change you;
only you,
can change your ways.

What is built can be broken;
but what is broken can be fixed.

External Pressure

I was just about to change myself
for the sake of pleasing others;
then I realised
I wouldn't really be living my life,
I'd be existing in someone else's narrative.

Part of You

When you died, you took half of me with you;
but part of you still lives on, within me.

Non-Commercialised Grief is Vaid

Do not think just because the person you've lost
is still alive, that you have no right to grieve that loss.

That loss is a different kind of passing;
that still leaves a gap in your heart that takes time to heal.
A feeling of confusion consumes your head
as you try to hold back the tears.

But when you're used to having someone in your life
and then one day they're not there,
it's tough to adjust to the reality of not having them around.

Regardless of the circumstances that lead to that person
no longer being in your life;
it's okay to feel lost,
you will find your way again.

Discomfort does not equal failure.

Shallow Assumptions

I stopped trying to be liked by everyone when I realised,
no matter what you do,
some people will make shallow assumptions of you.

Nor can you force anyone to see the parts of you
they turn a blind eye to.

Facial Hair

I thought you'd be repulsed by my lip hair;
that my untamed eyebrows,
would make you wince.

How silly of me to think,
that a few little hairs was all you'd see.
That they'd be enough, to put you off me.

Their existence,
has not morphed my entire face shape.

My beauty sits deeper
than unwaxed facial hair
on the surface of my skin.

Healing Is Messy

In an ideal world,
things would have panned out differently;
but I do not live in an ideal world.

I live in reality,
where healing is messy;
and you can still feel lost on the right path.

Even when things are going well,
life can still feel wrong
because of the sacrifices that were made.

But there are times where you have to let go,
in order to grow
beyond what you thought was possible.

The hardest decision can be the one
that sets you free.

Path of Change

I am on a journey towards change;
for once, I see the glorious path that lays out before me.

But then I feel a lump in my chest,
I feel my surroundings caving in and stop.

My vision becomes blurred, I lose sense of myself
and can barely see what's ahead.

I turn to find
all the younger versions of myself standing in a row
behind me.

Should I have stayed that way?
But then I see
the longing in my eyes for something more.

Despite my imperfect vision, I return my gaze forward
and see the outline,
of who I am yet to become;
aware there will be obstacles ahead, but I regain my focus.

A distant cheer
rises from behind me;
I turn to find everything I have been cheering me on.

'Don't stop now, keep going!' They say.
So, I continue forward
with the vision of who I will become,
at the forefront of my mind.

Taking with me the vigorous energy from my past,
that got me to where I am today.

Conversation with My Fifteen-Year-Old Self

There she is in front of me,
the girl I was at fifteen;
wearing black leggings and a cropped hoodie.
Somehow, in one summer
she's dimmed so much of who she is.

I can see the masked pain in her eyes;
but I know she's trying to make the most
of the situation she's in.
Spending her days escaping through music
and roaming through town after school,
with a hope of finding herself again.

She breaks the silence by asking, 'Does it get better?'
I want to tell her everything,
warn her about the changes that are about to happen;
but that will only panic her, so I refrain.

Knowing that nothing I say,
will make the next few years any easier;
and some things,
are better revealed with time.

So, I say,

'Stick to what you know is right;
do not let anyone tell you otherwise,
you will not see it straight away,
but things will get better.'

A subtle look of disbelief comes over her face,
I can understand why.
She may have asked the question,
but the idea of a better life seems like fantasy to her.

I reach out my hand
but she stands up from her chair, and opens up her arms.
This took me by surprise;
hugging is not something
that felt comfortable to her.

I follow her lead and rise from my chair,
to hug the girl I was;
I don't want to let go,
I want to take her with me.
Knowing what awaits her over the next few years.

But I know somehow, she'll be okay.
I know I am who I am today
because of what she is about to face.
I wasn't right;
it isn't what we deserved,
but I stand in front of her as woman;
the woman she is about to become.

Part Three: Hope

Hope is a thing with feathers, and she's tied by the wings.
Unable to fly past the crap that surrounds her;
unable to reach us at a time of need.

Without her sweet melodies singing songs of tomorrow;
it's hard to see a way out of today's sorrow.

We pray for the day she will break away
from the ties that constraint her;
and sing sweet songs once more,
to guide us through the eye of the storm.

[inspired by Emily Dickenson's 'hope']

My Body Is a Temple

My body is a temple;
I worship all that is within me, I am careful with who I let in.

A man may bow down at my feet;
but that does not always equal respect.
It can simply be a facade;
I won't give in to soulless flattery.

My body is a temple;
it deserves to be loved, not torn apart,
by a man who believes he owns me.

Words More Powerful Than 'I Love You'

I need you;
three words more powerful than 'I love you.'
You can love from a distance;
my need for you is a need for your presence.
I need you by me as you are,
nothing more, nothing less.

Soul Sister [For Eleanor]

When we hug,
time has always seemed to stand still;
it's our unspoken understanding.
We stand side by side,
stronger than what came before us,
with the universe at our feet.

You have a gleam
that brightens the dullest stage;
the world is lucky
to have you shining in it.

Lips Like Cherry Wine

Don't wait around
the suspense will kill us;
understand that to grab my hips is an honour,
kissing my lips,
is like drinking cherry wine on a summer's day;
and if you treat me right,
I'll let you stay.

Free from the Fear of Regret

I'd rather regret what I have done
and learn from my mistake;
then regret what I haven't done,
only to become a prisoner of endless what if's.

Love Is Nothing without Respect

You desire to be mine;
and if we build a foundation of mutual respect,
I have no doubt our love will be divine.
Like the wine produced
from the sweetest grapes on the vine.

Indomitable Spirit

I know who I am;
not just by name but by nature,
even on days I forgot,
my indomitable spirit remains.
Through all of life's trials,
it's the part of me that cannot be stolen;
the part of me that leads the way,
when my body feels lifeless.

Time Does Not Make Us Wiser

Age is merely a maker of time lived;
It gives no true insight
into if those years were utilised.
Time alone does not make you wiser;
it is how you spend that time that counts.

Home Is Where You Are

To me this house is not my home;
I am at home when I'm with you,
our love has built four walls of peace and a roof of trust.

When my head feels uneasy,
you give me a shoulder to rest it on,
and a sense of ease takes over.
Safe in the knowledge that when we're together,
I will always feel at home.

The Wink

You wouldn't think such a simple wink
would have such a hold on me;
everything that came before melted in that moment.
It hit me like a bullet; my heart surrented.

I thought this was the kind of meeting
that only happened in books,
in today's society
of online situation-ships;
but this felt like fate.
You looked right into my eyes and into my soul;
as though you could read my deepest thoughts.

Everyone around us dissipated into oblivion;
afterwards I thought,
So that is what
love at first sight feels like.

Bubble Wrapped Love

Talking to someone
you are beginning to fall for,
is like being raped in bubble wrap
and being pushed down the stairs;
but they're there at the bottom,
to catch you every time.

Water and Blood

If blood is family,
then friendship is water;
blood may be thicker,
but it cannot flow without water, both are vital.

Raise Them Higher

This is where it ends,
my children will not carry the weight of my past.

I cannot protect them from all they will face;
but I will make sure they know
just how important they are.

Not only though my words but in my actions;
be the parent I needed, the adult they need.

Raise them high enough to see,
a world that is theirs
to succeed in.

Loveable

Just because one person failed to love you
in the way you deserved,
does not mean it's impossible.

Believe me when I say:
You are loved;
and you are worthy of receiving that love.

Destine

Go out there and claim the life
you were told you could never have;
the life that was destined to be yours.
You may not know what that looks like yet,
but it awaits you.

Something Wonderful

This could all be a mistake;
but I won't know that until I try.
If I do not step into the unknown from time to time,
I am not truly living;
I would simply be alive.

I want to feel alive;
I want to navigate through fear,
not coast in comfort
just because it's comfortable.

The comfort I feel
does not mean it is good for me;
I could be one decision away
from something wonderful.

Disguised Joy

Sometimes you don't know it was what you needed
until you're experiencing it;
sometimes life's greatest joy's,
disguise themselves as a pit of terror in your stomach.

Fever Dream

I've been revisiting the places we used to,
in the hopes of dissolving the trauma that lingers there;
detaching you from the places we used to go.

It has been filled with moments
where I thought you were behind me;
I would be lying if I said,
the distress was gone completely.
Occasionally, a trigger will appear.

But I put it in the past where it belongs;
I take a deep inhale,
remind myself:
I am safe and exhale
into the present moment in time;
where you
will never reach me.

The triggers are weakening with time;
the memory of you,
is beginning to feel like a fever dream.

Unitentunal Meditations

There I sat under the sunrise,
and closed my eyes.
At first, a few thoughts crossed my mind
but then my mind silenced,
I became unbothered by all that surrounded me;
very little entered my head space,
I allowed myself to let go of time.

I used to be afraid of silence; it was always too loud,
my head would flood with worry.
I would feel myself drowning,
in the panic, my thoughts invoked.

But in that moment
neither the past nor future could reach me;
my focus was devoted to the present.
I had a non-verbal realisation
of the peace that is within me;
that my busy brain often hides.
I remained awake; as I opened my eyes,
I felt as though I had a full night's rest.

Empathy

We don't have to experience the same of pain, to empathise with others.

Gorgeous

In the past,
I've flown high, too fast
only to crash and burn;
but why rush,
when we could have a lifetime together before us?

There's something gorgeous in the mystery
of what's to come.

I can be content with my life
and still strive towards change.

Life Is Colour

Life is colour;
when born we are raped in white,
to symbolise a new beginning
a life yet to be lived.

Life itself is
red, blue, purple, green
and all the other colours in between.

And when we die,
the people we loved dress in black,
to symbolise the life of colour we led.

Undress My Mind

Even with my clothes off, I am not naked;
it is when you undress my mind, that I am truly bare.

When you see what lies beneath the surface of my body,
unveiled are my thoughts and faults,
my strengths and struggles.
You will see all that I am, everything I am not
and catch a glimpse of who I will become.

Tranquillity

As I sit in silence, my soul rejuvenates;
a rare occurrence in this world that is consistently in a rush.

In reality nothing can ever be truly silent;
distance sounds can still be heard,
but that almost adds to the tranquillity,
since they do not have my full attention.

I am to focused on how I feel in this percent moment
to be concerned about the happenings beyond my windows.

The past Cannot Reach You Here

You are here in the present, you are safe;
I know they've hurt you,
but the strain of your past can not reach you here.

Nothing Can Return to Nothing

I was frightened by the idea off your heart failing to beat;
but death is a part of nature and nothing to fear.
The thought alone
does not make the pain of your passing dissipate,
or make me miss you less.
But I reminded myself:
Nothing can come from nothing;
therefore, nothing can return to nothing.

The bodies we are in are merely a vessel
for us to live our lives;
when we pass, we will always
leave a part of ourselves behind.
This reassures me that you are with me;
not in a physical sense,
but the love you had for me remains.
I will carry on your spirit
and live my life as you intended me to.

Old-Fashioned Love Narrative

It's an old-fashioned way of thinking:
A woman with a man is weakened;
and when I find my person, I lose half of myself.
The statement feels like a misjudgement
of just how strong a woman can be.

It's just feeding the narrative that as a woman,
I have no mind of my own; I must obey.
I find it hard to believe the right person
will make me feeble out of the blue.
If they do in fact make me feel less than,
they are not who I want to spend my life with.

Self-Love Is Not a Threat

The self-love I possess
does not pose as a threat to society;
nor is it some form of toxic vanity.

It will not diminish my ability to love others,
or be mistaken for an inflated ego.
For the more love I have for myself,
the more I'll have to give.

Without self-love
I would be plagued by disconnection from within,
unable to create deep and meaningful connections.

I'll Be Your Refuge

When you feel miles away,
I'll bring you back down to Earth;
when you get lost in confusion,
I'll help you navigate through it.

I will be your refuge
when you need a place to rest,
for you deserve the very best.

Thoughts Are like Bees

I don't know how I feel;
but I know what I don't feel.

I feel neither happy nor sad: I am simply sat in stillness,
observing without much thought;
stripping my surroundings down,
finding shelter in my soul.

A bee has flown in front of my face.
I think to myself:
Should I move?
But I know if I don't get myself into a state of panic,
it will not sting me.
If I maintain this calm demeanour, it will fly away
to continue collecting pollen
for the sweetest honey ever tasted.

Thoughts have a similar nature to the bee;
the conscience of our thoughts is determined
by how or if we act on them.
This action or inaction could be the difference
between a thought leaving a string or,
producing sweet honey in our lifetime.

Crushed by a Sea of People

I caught myself walking around like a soulless zombie,
in the muggy city air;
I watched as people crammed themselves onto the tube,
like cattle on a meat farm.

I was nothing more than one fish,
making my way through an unbearable current;
as my body became smothered by the crowd,
my head escaped to the sea.

I thought of the crashing of waves,
as a sea of people crashed against me.
Like I was rock on a cliff face,
slowly eroding.

I fear this way of life
will continue to chip away at my soul,
until there's nothing left of me.

A new way of life is calling me.

17:17

We have been talking on the phone for a few hours now.
I am still outside; my hands are starting to freeze.

The connection cuts off when I go into my hallway,
so I remain outside.
With you at the other end of the line,
I cannot really feel the cold;
our conversation keeps me warm,
your voice is a comfort to me.

The clock just turned 17:17,
this is a chance for a beautiful new beginning;
a door once blocked, has been opened,
to reconnect with those I love the most.

I walk in from the cold
after another two hours on the phone,
with warmth in my heart.
You made feel a sense of joy I haven't felt in weeks;
you have always brought me peace.

Regrowth

When I began to crumble,
you placed out your hands out beneath me
and collected
every
last
piece.

You did not let
a single ounce of me, get swept away;
you found me a place
where I could grow.

When Silver Is Worth More than Gold

Who decided gold
was worth more than silver?
For if I prefer silver,
surly it holds more value
to me than gold.

Body Language

Dance
is a language
that uses no words;
it is a way of communicating using only,
the sensual movement of my hips.

As they sway
and roll to the music,
a sense of freedom takes over me.

Risen as a Woman

You may have raised me to be a girl;
but I have risen
as a woman.

Tables Turning

You saw my weakness,
and used it as your strength.

When in fact, your corruption
makes you the weaker one, and me a whole lot stronger.

Comfort

Let my words rap
around you, like silk.

Coffee at 8 p.m.

We'd go to Bella's for dinner, and order a margarita pizza, half with olives; half without;
and talk about all that was on our minds.

By eight p.m., we'd be drinking coffee,
God only knows why
we thought that was a good idea.

By nine p.m., we'd be laughing around Tesco without a care,
and that dead town would dissipate.
I'd only known you three months;
but it felt like we'd been friends for a lifetime.

If I haven't told you before, I am proud of you
and honoured to call you my friend.
This goes without saying,
but never forget the value,
you add to this world.

New Moon

New moon,
fresh start.

A fresh start leads to the possibility,
of newfound joy.

Falsehoods fall in the moonlight;
a new way of life is revealed,
after the dawn,
this journey will continue in sunlight.

A dark past does not mean,
a bright future cannot be found.

In all her glory, the moon reminds me
that even she,
keeper of the night sits upon a blue sky
from time to time.

Comfortable Silence

Here we are
in a comfortable silence, knowing what needs to be said
will be shared in time.

But in this moment,
we are bathing in the bliss of each other's company.

As I lay in your arms, I let your affection,
seep into my bones.

Complete,
I am not afraid to love any more.